Béisbol! Latino Heroes of Major League Baseball

JOSE Altuve

JOSH LEVENTHAL

Bolt is published by Black Rabbit Books
P.O. Box 3263, Mankato, Minnesota, 56002.
www.blackrabbitbooks.com

Design and Production by Michael Sellner
Photo Research by Rhonda Milbrett

Library of Congress Control Number: 2015954850

HC ISBN: 978-1-68072-044-0 PB ISBN: 978-1-68072-302-1

Printed in the United States at CG Book Printers,
North Mankato, Minnesota, 56003. PO #1797 4/16

Image Credits

Alamy: Tribune Content Agency LLC, 16; AP Images: BOB LEVEY, 3, 21; Kathy Willens, 4–5; Mike Janes, 10, 13; Ted S. Warren, 17 (bottom); Corbis: Mike McGinnis/ZUMA Press, 14; Getty: Denis Poroy/Stringer, Cover; Victor Decolongon, 8–9; meridiano.com.ve: Foto Archivo, 18; Shutterstock: CarpathianPrince, 28–29 (ball); DVARG, 9 (rackets); Eugene Onischenko, 24–25 (background); Joe Belanger, 24–25 (bat); karawan, 8 (hand); Marie C Fields, 31; Mc LOVIN, 8 (scale); Palokha Tetiana, 19; vasosh, 14, 24 (ball), 28, 29; USA Today: Ed Szczepanski, 17 (top); FR156786 AP, 32; Joe Camporeale, 23; Peter Aiken, 28–29 (background); Tim Heitman, 26; Troy Taormina, Back Cover, 1, 7
Every effort has been made to contact copyright holders for material reproduced in this book. Any omissions will be rectified in subsequent printings if notice is given to the publisher.

Contents

TPX

CHAPTER 1

A Latino

Jose Altuve steps up to the plate. He watches the pitcher closely. The ball sails toward him. Altuve drives the ball to deep left-center field. He takes off around the bases. He speeds past first base. He rounds second base. He gets to third and keeps on running. Altuve crosses home plate. It's an inside-the-park home run!

Short but Skilled

Altuve is an all-star baseball player. His batting skills are some of the best. He's also great at stealing bases. And he's an excellent second-base player.

But Altuve wasn't always a pro ball player. He grew up in Venezuela. He loved baseball. But he was always smaller than the other kids. Coaches and **scouts** told him he was too small to play baseball. Altuve proved them wrong.

Fun Facts

right handed

WEIGHT

165 POUNDS (75 kilograms)

5 feet, 5 inches (1.7 m) tall

Altuve is the shortest player in the major leagues.

His nickname is "gigante." It means "giant" in Spanish.

plays table tennis with his teammates

2'

1'

0

CHAPTER 2

A Young Baseball Star

Altuve was born May 6, 1990. Young Altuve had great **reflexes** and was very fast.

At age 16, he went to a Houston Astros tryout in Venezuela. He was barely over 5 feet (1.5 m) tall. The scouts told him to go home. They thought he was too small. But Altuve didn't quit. He went back the next day and played well. The Astros were impressed. They soon signed Altuve to a contract.

Working in the Minors

In 2007, Altuve played for the Venezuelan Summer League Astros. He had a batting average of .343. That was the best on the team.

Altuve came to the United States in 2008. He played for the Greeneville Astros. He was named the team's Most Valuable Player (MVP) in 2009.

Number of Latino Major League Baseball Players

through 2015

642	Dominican Republic
341	Venezuela
253	Puerto Rico
193	Cuba
118	Mexico
55	Panama
17	Colombia
14	Curacao
14	Nicaragua
12	U.S. Virgin Islands
6	Bahamas
5	Aruba
4	Jamaica
3	Brazil
1	Belize
1	Honduras

CHAPTER 3

In the Majors

In 2011, Altuve continued to shine in the **minor leagues**. In July, the Astros brought him to the major leagues. He got a base hit in each of his first seven games. Altuve hit his first Major League Baseball (MLB) home run on August 20. It was an inside-the-park homer to start the game.

Becoming an All-Star

Altuve led the Astros with a .290 average in 2012. He used his speed to steal 33 bases and score 80 **runs**. Those numbers were the highest on the team too. Altuve was chosen for that year's All-Star Game.

Eye on the Ball

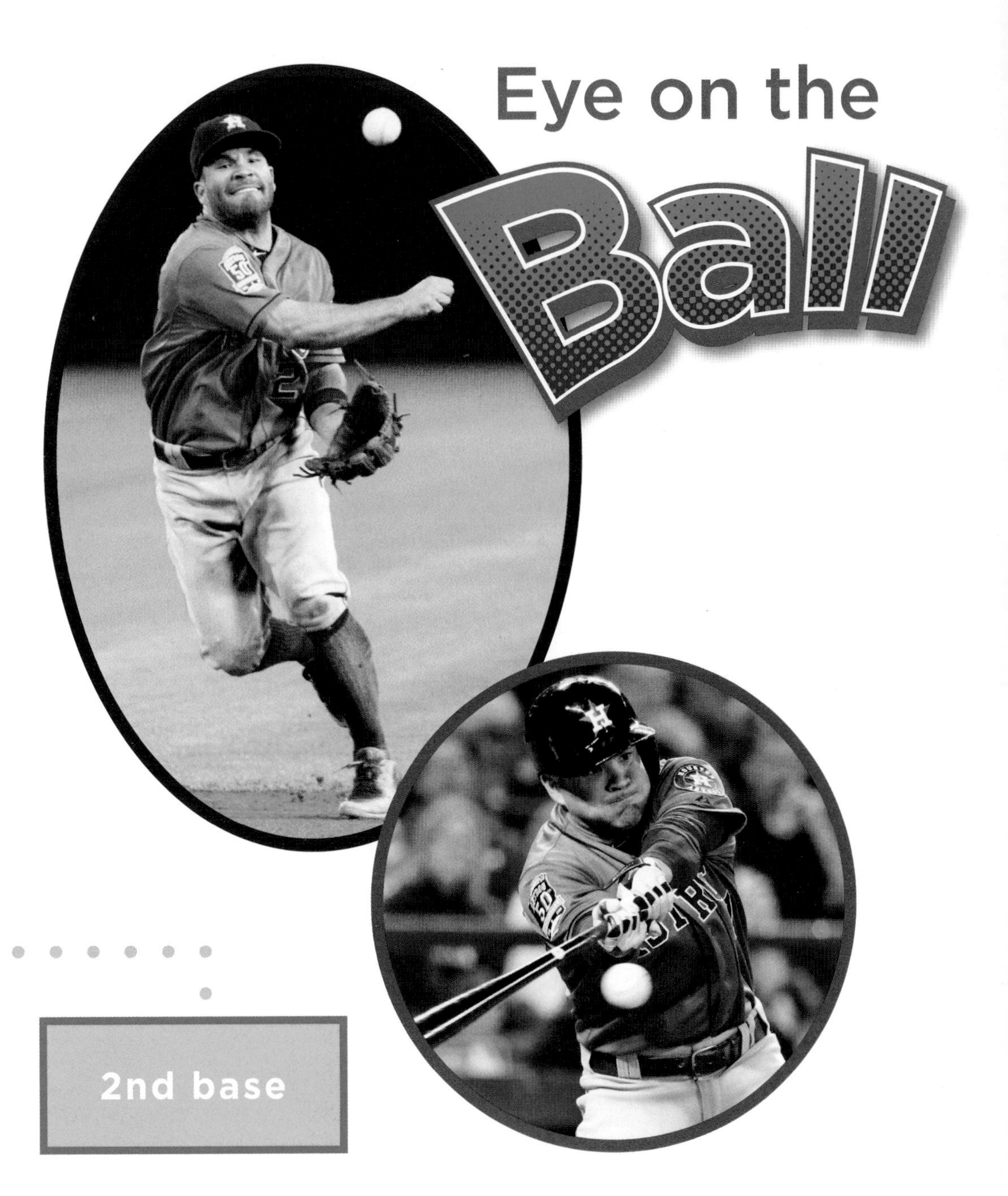

Winter Ball in Venezuela

Between seasons, Altuve went home to Venezuela. He played in the winter league from 2010 to 2012. He wanted to keep working and improving. Altuve batted .339 in 2011. He had a .336 average in 2012. He led his teams in hitting both years.

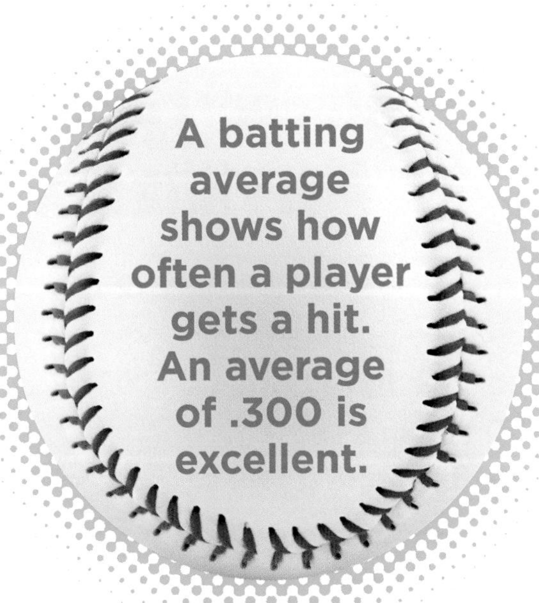

Big Money

In 2013, Altuve signed a new contract with Houston. The Astros promised to pay him $12.5 million over four years. The team saw him as a leader and a top star. At only 23 years old, Altuve was one of the best second basemen in MLB.

Venezuelan Players with 200 or More Hits in a Season

Only three players from Venezuela have gotten 200 hits in a season. Altuve has done it twice.

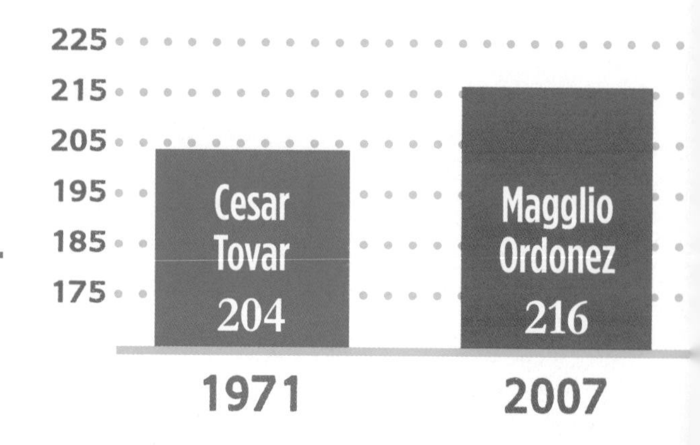

ASTROS
Jose
Altuve
225
2014
Jose
Altuve
200
2015

CHAPTER 4

Continuing to

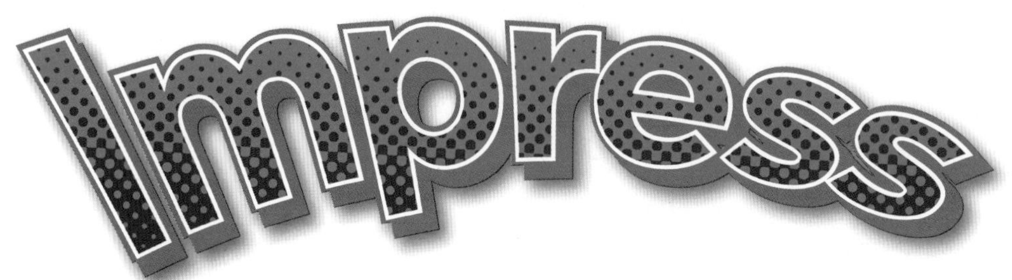

Altuve had his best season yet in 2014. He had the highest batting average in MLB. He became the first Astro ever to win a batting title. Altuve also set an all-time team record with 225 hits. His 56 stolen bases were the most in the **American League**.

Most Stolen Bases from 2011–2015

Dee Gordon **188**

Rajai Davis **179**

Ben Revere	Jose Altuve	Jacoby Ellsbury
176	169	165

Games Played

2011 **57**

2012 **147**

2013 **152**

2014 **158**

2015 **154**

Runs

2011 2012 2013 2014 2015

Hits

61
2011

167
2012

177
2013

Stolen Bases

2011

2012

2013

2014

2015

Batting Average

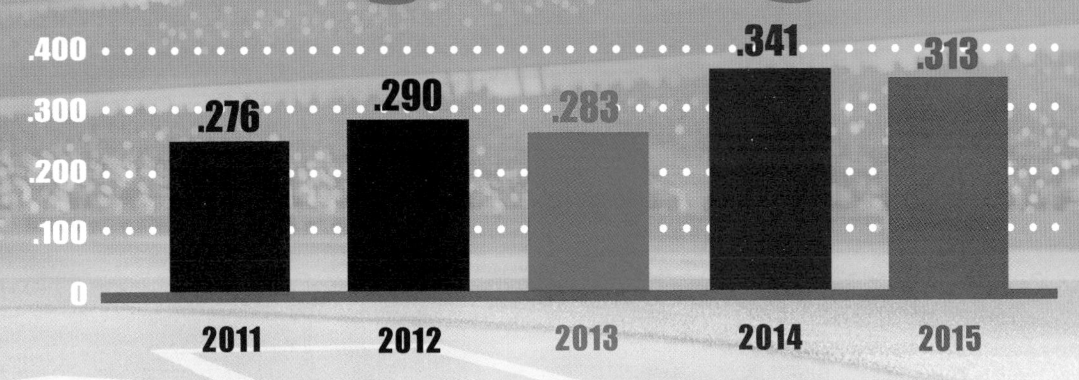

225
2014

200
2015

Jose Altuve (2011-2015)	vs	Craig Biggio (1988-1992)
830	Hits	624
36	Home Runs	30
169	Stolen Bases	109

Powerful Player

Many people compare Altuve to Craig Biggio. Biggio was Houston's second baseman from 1988 to 2007. Biggio is in the Baseball Hall of Fame. Altuve's early career is similar to his.

Jose Altuve continues to get better. He was an All-Star in three of his first four full seasons. He gets a lot of hits and steals bases. He is also a great fielder. Altuve is a powerful player. And fans love him.

Timeline

1990

May

Altuve is born.

2006

March

signs with the Houston Astros

2007

plays first minor league game

2011

July

plays first major league game

2014

wins Silver Slugger award

wins American League batting title

2015

wins Silver Slugger and Gold Glove

October

gets first postseason hit

GLOSSARY

American League (uh-MER-i-can LEEG)—one of two groups that make up Major League Baseball in the United States; the American League champion plays the National League champion in the World Series each year.

Latino (luh-TEE-no)—from Mexico or a country in South America, Central America, or the Caribbean

minor league (MY-nur LEEG)—a professional baseball organization that competes at levels below the major leagues

postseason (POST-see-zuhn)—games played after the regular season

reflex (REE-flecks)—something a person does without thinking as a reaction to something

run (RUN)—when a player safely crosses home plate before the team has three outs

scout (SKOWT)—a person sent to get information about someone or something

BOOKS

Dobrow, Larry. *Derek Jeter's Ultimate Baseball Guide 2015*. New York: Little Simon, 2015.

Kelley, K. C. *Baseball Superstars 2015*. New York: Scholastic Paperback Nonfiction, 2015.

Stewart, Mark. *The Houston Astros*. Team Spirit. Chicago: Norwood House Press, 2012.

WEBSITES

Baseball
www.ducksters.com/sports/baseball.php

Jose Altuve
m.mlb.com/player/514888/jose-altuve

Official Houston Astros Website
houston.astros.mlb.com/index.jsp?c_id=hou

INDEX